MW01505064

WHO STARTED WORLD WAR 1?

History 6th Grade
Children's Military Books

BABY PROFESSOR
EDUCATION KIDS

Speedy Publishing LLC

40 E. Main St. #1156

Newark, DE 19711

www.speedypublishing.com

Copyright 2017

World War I was the major conflict that was fought between 1914 and 1918. It was also referred to as WWI, the First World War, the Great War, and the War to End All Wars. In this book, we will be learning about the start of the war, how it was fought, and how it ended.

WHO FOUGHT IN WORLD WAR I?

WWI was fought between what was known as the Central Powers and what was known as the Allied Powers. The Allied Powers were comprised mainly of Russia, Britain and France. After 1917, the United States fought with the Allies. The Central Powers were comprised mainly of Bulgaria, Germany, Austria-Hungry and the Ottoman Empire.

Great War Memorial in Lille

Observation Post at Fort Douaumont

WHERE DID MOST OF THE FIGHTING OCCUR?

Most of the war occurred along two separate fronts in Europe: the eastern front and the western front. The eastern front was between Bulgaria, Austria-Hungary, and Germany on one side and on the other side consisted of Russia and Romania.

Trenches of World War I

The western front consisted of a long line of trenches running from Switzerland to the coast of Belgium. Much of the fighting occurred in Belgium and France.

Archduke Franz Ferdinand

HOW DID THE WAR BEGIN?

While there were many causes for the war, the main catalyst for starting it was the assassination of Franz Ferdinand, the Austrian Archduke. After this assassination took place, Austria decided to declare war on Serbia. Russia then prepared to defend Serbia, its ally.

Germany then declared war on Russia in order to protect Austria. This then made France declare war on Germany to protect Russia, who was its ally. Germany then proceeded to invade Belgium in order to get to France, causing Britain to declare war on Germany. All of this took place in only a few days.

Trenches and Craters on Battlefield of Vimy ridge

Trench Soldier

MAJOR BATTLES

Most of WWI was fought along the western front in what was known as trench warfare and the armies barely moved at all. They would simply bomb and shoot at each other from across these trenches. The First Battle of the Marne, Battle of Tannenberg, Battle of the Somme, Battle of Verdun, and the Battle of Gallipoli were some of the major battles during this war.

THE END OF THE WAR

On November 11, 1918, the fighting ended once both sides agreed to a general armistice. It officially ended once the Treaty of Versailles was signed between Germany and the Allies.

Treaty of Versailles Signing

The arrest of Gavrilo Prinzep, assassin of Austrian Archduke Franz Ferdinand

CAUSES OF WW1

As discussed earlier, there were several factors leading up to the beginning of WWI in Europe. Many were rooted deep into the history of the older European powers such as Germany, Russia, Italy, France, Hungary, Austria and Britain. Secret alliances, politics, nationalistic pride, and imperialism were some of the real causes of this war. The assassination of Austria's Archduke Ferdinand was, however, the one single event leading to WWI.

ALLIANCES AND POLITICS

During the time period leading up the WWI, European nations were jockeying for power constantly and making alliances. In 1881, Germany made an alliance with Italy and Austria-Hungary and they agreed to protect one another should they find themselves under attack by France. Italy, however, proceeded to make a secret alliance with France agreeing they would not aide Germany.

Battle of the Tannenberg

Czar Nicholas II and French General Joffre

In 1892, Russia and France became allies in response to Germany's alliances. France and Britain signed an agreement in 1904. Russia, France, and Britain formed the Triple Entente in 1907. Germany believed that the powerful alliance that surrounded them would pose a major threat to their power and existence in the region.

IMPERIALISM

When a country's power and influence expands to a large empire, it is referred to as Imperialism. Some countries in Europe, such as Britain and France created large empires worldwide and became quite rich. Other countries, including Germany and Russia, wanted to build their own empires. This created conflict and competition between several countries around the world.

Czar Nicholas II and French General Joffre

READY FOR WAR

In 1914, the situation was tense in Europe. Internal politics, secret alliances, and a desire to build empires had created dislike and distrust between several European powers. It would only take one international event and Europe would then be at war.

ASSASSINATION OF ARCHDUKE FERDINAND

Archduke Franz Ferdinand, the heir to the Austria-Hungary empire, was assassinated on June 28, 1914 in Sarajevo. The government of Austria thought that this assassination had been organized by the Serbian government and they believed this to be an opportunity to regain control over Serbia.

Assassination of Archduke Franz Ferdinand

Battlefield Trench

DECLARING WAR

Austria-Hungary proceeded to issue many demands on Serbia, threatening invasion if Serbia would not comply with these demands, giving them 48 hours within which to respond. Once Serbia's response fell short, Austria-Hungary, on July 28, declared war on Serbia.

ADDITIONAL DECLARATIONS OF WAR

Austria-Hungary hoped they would be able to take over Serbia quickly and that Russia, Serbia's ally, would take risk a major war to assist Serbia. However, they were wrong, and Russia started immediately mobilizing their troops and preparing for war.

Russian Troops

Russian Troops

Germany, in response, as Austria-Hungary's close ally, on August 1 declared war on Russia. Germany declared war on France a few days later and invaded Belgium. Britain proceeded to declare war on Germany and this was the beginning of World War I.

THE BLAME

Over the years, historians have tried to understand who really was to blame for starting this war. Today, many agree that it was Germany that wanted to start it. The leaders of Germany believed they were surrounded by enemies, including Russia and France, and that eventually war was going to take place. They believed that the sooner war occurred, the better chance Germany had for winning.

German Infantry

German Troops

TRENCH WARFARE

The type of fighting when each side builds a deep trench as a defense against the enemy is known as trench warfare. They might stretch for several miles which makes it almost impossible for one side to advance.

In France, the western front was fought using trench warfare during World War I. Both sides had constructed trenches by the end of 1914 that stretched from the North Sea and through France and Belgium. Neither side was able to gain much ground from October of 1914 to March of 1918.

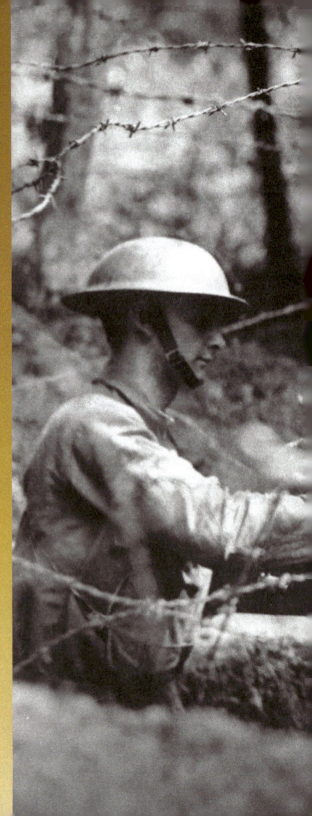

World War 1 Trenches

HOW DID THEY BUILD THE TRENCHES?

Soldiers dug the trenches and often they simply dug them straight in the ground. This was known as entrenching. While it was quick to dig the trenches, it left them open to enemy fire as they were digging. They would sometimes build them by extending one end of the trench. This was known as sapping. It took longer, but it was safer. The safest way to build it was by making a tunnel and then removing the roof once the tunnel was complete. While tunneling was the most difficult method, it was the safest.

NO MAN'S LAND

Land located between two enemy trench lines was referred to as "No Man's Land" and would sometimes be covered with land mines and barbed wire. Generally, the trenches of the enemy would be separated by approximately 50 to 250 yards.

No Man's Land

Vimy Ridge Trench

WHAT WERE THEY LIKE?

Typically, a trench would be dug about 12 feet deep in the ground and at the top of it would be an embankment as well as a barbed wire fence. Sometimes the trenches would be reinforced with sandbags or wooden beams and the bottom was typically covered with wood boards known as duckboards. These duckboards were intended to keep the soldiers' feet above water that collected towards the bottom of the trench.

They were not dug in a straight line, but rather built more like a system of trenches. They would be dug in a zigzag patter and there would be several trench levels along the lines and had paths dug for the soldiers to travel between these levels.

World War 1 Trench

LIVING IN THE TRENCHES

Typically, soldiers would rotate through three different stages at the front. They spent some time at the front-line of the trenches, some of their time at the support trenches, and some of the time resting. They would almost always have some type of job to perform, whether it was guard duty, repairing the trenches, undergoing inspections, cleaning their weapons or moving supplies.

CONDITIONS IN THE TRENCHES

Trenches were not clean, nice places and they were actually very disgusting. There would be all types of pests including lice, frogs and rats. The rats would be everywhere and even get in the soldiers' food and eat just about all of it. Lice were also a big problem by making them itch horribly and caused the disease known as Trench Fever.

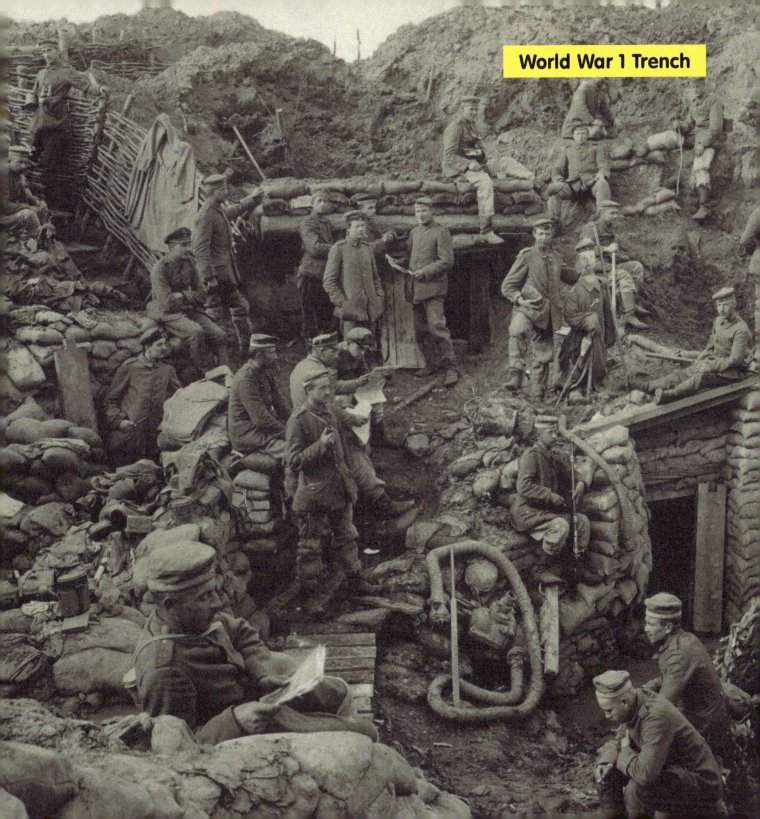

World War 1 Trench

Weather would also contribute to the rough conditions. Rain would cause flooding and muddiness and the mud would clog the weapons and make it difficult to move during battle.

Additionally, constant moisture in the trenches would cause Trench Foot, an infection that if left untreated could become so bad that their foot would have to be amputated. The cold weather was also dangerous and soldiers would often lose toes or fingers to frostbite and some actually died from exposure to the cold weather.

WWI Verdun Military Cemetery

Known as one of history's largest wars, more than nine million combatants lost their lives as a result of this war, as well as seven million civilians that included victims of genocides.

For additional information about World War I you can go to your local library, research the internet, and ask questions of your teachers, family, and friends.

The Vimy World War One Canadian Memorial in France

Visit

BABY PROFESSOR
EDUCATION KIDS

www.BabyProfessorBooks.com

to download Free Baby Professor eBooks
and view our catalog of new and exciting
Children's Books

CPSIA information can be obtained
at www.ICGtesting.com
Printed in the USA
BVHW012255130222
628923BV00022BA/423